On Angel's Wings
A Miraculous Survival
By Dr. Robert L. Black

Published in Columbia, South Carolina, by KB&G LLC Publishers & Booksellers.

All scripture quotations are taken from the New Revised Standard Version Updated Edition of the Holy Bible.
ISBN 10- 8890908297
ISBN 13- 9798890908292

Printed in the United States of America

This book is dedicated to
those who are facing a hard situation and you
are waiting to see God become the one that
declares, "There is nothing too hard for me!"

CONTENTS

Preface 04

Introduction 06

Chapter 1-Miracles? 11

Chapter 2-From the start 15

Chapter 3-The Prayer Walk that Changed Everything 23

Chapter 4-An Angels Wings Experience 27

Chapter 5-The Miracle of Movement 35

Chapter 6-Closing Message 43

Other books by author 51

Preface

As a reader delving into this extraordinary account, I am both humbled and astounded by the miraculous events that unfolded on that fateful day. The story you are about to read is nothing short of remarkable. It recounts the miraculous survival of the author, who, while out for an ordinary walk, became the victim of an unforeseen and near-fatal accident.

Picture this: an ordinary day with clear skies, the kind of day where one would expect nothing more than a peaceful stroll. However, destiny had other plans. An out-of-control car came hurtling towards him, striking with such force that he was literally knocked out of his shoes. By all accounts, he should have perished. The severity of his injuries and the grim statistics of similar accidents made survival seem impossible. Yet, against all odds, he lived.

The author's survival is a testament to the power of miracles. It defies logic and challenges our understanding of life and death. Hearing about the extent of his injuries and knowing how many people have succumbed to such accidents only deepens the sense of awe. This preface is an invitation to read on and witness, through his words, the undeniable presence of a higher power at work.

As you turn these pages, prepare to be inspired by a narrative that transcends the ordinary. This book is not just about a close brush with death; it is a celebration of resilience, faith, and the inexplicable forces that guide us. May this story of miraculous survival fill your heart with hope and reaffirm your belief in the extraordinary.

Hugh J. Harmon

Introduction

Life often has a way of surprising us in the most unexpected and profound manners. Certain events can leave a lasting impression, shaping our perception of the world and our place within it. One such event in my life was an accident that could have ended tragically but instead demonstrated the resilience of the human spirit and the possibility of encountering miracles even in the darkest moments.

Some people view miracles as illusions or trickery, while others regard them as manifestations of faith. The Bible describes faith as "the substance of things hoped for, the evidence of things not yet seen." It is often said that expectation sets the stage for miracles, yet there are instances where miracles occur without any anticipation.

God is known as the God of miracles. His miraculous acts are documented both in the

Old Testament and the New Testament. While we may not witness parting seas or raising individuals from the dead today, it is believed that God continues to perform miracles in our everyday lives.

As followers of Christ, we may experience miracles frequently. According to the Gospel of Mark, "These signs shall follow them that believe," suggesting that supernatural phenomena will accompany those who truly believe in Jesus Christ. Observable acts such as healing the sick or casting out demons are considered miraculous, indicating that a faithful believer's life should be characterized by miracles.

This book aims to recount one such miracle that occurred unexpectedly, outside the realm of immediate expectation. I did not anticipate the danger I faced, nor did I foresee the miraculous outcome that followed.

The notion that "goodness and mercy" shall follow us all the days of our lives holds true, as evidenced by my survival of the incident. This narrative serves as a testament to that dynamic combination at work on that fateful day, allowing me to share this experience.

Miracles often inspire hope, strengthen faith, provide comfort during difficult times, demonstrate God's love and intervention, and bring about tangible positive changes, such as healing or provision. They encourage belief in something greater than us and living with more purpose. This book aims to tell a true story of an extraordinary experience within a relatively ordinary life that demonstrates the existence of a supernatural force, whom we call God, working on our behalf.

My hope is that your faith will be strengthened after reading about this remarkable experience. Although you may not have been a direct eyewitness, I trust that simply reading about it will stir something within you. Witnessing or believing in miracles can foster a stronger connection to a higher power, reinforcing faith and trust in a divine plan.

In times of hardship or despair, the concept of miracles can offer solace and the belief that positive change is possible, even in seemingly bleak circumstances. On that day, as the incident unfolded, I feared my life was over and anticipated future hardship and despair. However, that was not the outcome.

While many may dismiss modern-day miracles as fictitious, there are genuine miracles occurring daily, though they may not be reported in the media. These miracles are performed by God, as He is the God of miracles. From a woman deciding against abortion to a man choosing not to end his life, these acts are also miracles from God. Even if these individuals do not know Jesus as their Savior and Lord, He may be reaching out to them. Through reading about this unreported yet memorable miracle, I hope God reaches out to you as well.

Chapter One
Miracles?

Acts 3:16

And his name—by faith in his name—has made this man strong whom you see and know, and the faith that is through Jesus has given the man this perfect health in the presence of you all.

Do miracles still happen? This is a question that is continually asked and debated among us from the earliest days of people developing some level of faith in a divine being. From a Christian worldview the answer is simple, "Yes, He does! And He is doing it at the same frequency as it was being done in biblical times. Hebrews 13:8 tells us that Jesus Christ is the same yesterday, today and forevermore. God does miracles today just like in biblical times; we just don't hear about them, see them, or attribute them to him. If Jesus Christ could perform miracles two thousand years ago, he still can today. His heart broke for those hurting then, so it still does now. His desire to heal never changes. He's the same yesterday, today, and tomorrow. describes a compassionate God who wants to get involved even though he doesn't have to. Yes, he's proven himself, but he can't help loving us and refuses to sit back and do nothing. Who's to say with seven billion people on the planet that God hasn't done something miraculous in every one of those lives at some time, through someone, with something no one can explain, maybe even right now? It all depends on how you define a miracle.

Miracles are often described as instances of divine intervention in human affairs. They are also defined as highly unusual or outstanding events, things, or accomplishments. These occurrences often lead people, especially those who rely on logic, to question their nature. Some believe that miracles exist today, based on personal experiences and accounts from firsthand witnesses. The media may refer to these events as coincidences or chance, but others attribute them to a higher power. The belief is that divine intervention plays a role in the world today, though perhaps not to the same extent as historical accounts suggest. The Gospel of John states:

Jesus performed many other signs in the presence of his disciples, which are not recorded in this book. But these are written that you may believe that Jesus is the Messiah, the Son of God, and that by believing you may have life in his name. – John 20:30-31

Ever wonder about the miracles not included in the Gospels? They might have been subtle displays of power that didn't get much attention but were still miraculous. God still operates similarly today.

A miracle is when God intervenes in life's natural events, big or small. He inspires ideas, changes wind directions, influences markets, and stops traffic. This book aims to inspire you to believe in the miraculous God I serve. I want to share a miracle from my life that transformed my view of Him. I hope this true story will inspire you to believe that God still works miracles.

Troy Schmidt from his book, *Fish Sandwiches: The Delight of Receiving God's Promises God's power has never changed. The God that made thousands of miraculous fish sandwiches has the same power to work in new, quiet, and unexpected ways in your life today. Don't expect them. Don't demand them. Look for them. Know that if God wants to miraculously make you a sandwich or weave a basket or find you a job or cure your illness or find your prodigal son or fix your marriage, he can.*

Chapter Two
From the Start

2 Corinthians 4:8-10
We are hard pressed on every side, yet not crushed; we are perplexed, but not in despair; persecuted, but not forsaken; struck down, but not destroyed — always carrying about in the body the dying of the Lord Jesus, that the life of Jesus also may be manifested in our body

A famous gospel singer and author, Wintley Phipps once said, "It is in the quiet crucible of your personal private sufferings that your noblest dreams are born, and God's greatest gifts are given in compensation for what you've been through." How can a crucible be quiet? First, we must define the crucible. A crucible is a vessel of a very refractory material (such as porcelain) used for melting and calcining a substance that requires a high degree of heat.

In other words, crucibles take a beating and keep on ticking. Crucibles are analogous to any situation where things are lost, but the material of subject of attention is not destroyed but is made more durable.

Another powerful understanding that we need to have of a crucible is that often times, when things are placed in a crucible and go through the process of purification by fire that takes place in a crucible, the thing, be it a precious metal alloy, or some ore with a valuable mineral in its core–they always come out looking smaller or less than when they went in. Why? This is because the process that this object or item goes through in the crucible removes excess and leaves only that which is pure. In the context that Mr. Phipps was referring to, a crucible means the place of struggle and severe pain and is a bridge to a new beginning.

The events of July 4th, 2020, stand out as a significant day of profound struggle and pain for me, ultimately resulting in a life-changing experience. Although the day began like any other, by its end it marked an extraordinary turning point. I believe this was a moment of divine intervention, offering me a chance at a new beginning.

Throughout my life, I have encountered numerous transformative experiences which could be described as "rebirths." Moving from elementary school to middle school in Los Angeles, California, stands out as one such pivotal period. Another notable instance was when I embraced my faith as a young boy, although that was more of a spiritual rebirth rather than a physical one.

However, the rebirth I refer to here involves the remarkable restoration of my physical body, something that many would deem both impossible and implausible. This event transcends ordinary experiences, venturing into the realm of the miraculous. Experiencing the brink of death and subsequently being revived with newfound vitality provided a profound and life-altering perspective. Here, I aim to share the powerful testimony of divine healing.

On July 4th, 2020, my life transformed forever. That Saturday morning amid a worldwide pandemic with thousands upon thousands of lives perishing because of the dreaded COVID-19 outbreak, a divine miracle happened. Again, miracles are most powerfully observed and discerned in situations that shine a light on how impossible it seems. For example, the miracle of Jesus turning water into wine when you look at it from a purely westernized worldview was great. But when you realize that the water pots used were filled with water to clean the dust and dirt off the feet of the wedding guests, and you consider that the Governor of the feast remarked that the wedding party had chosen to share the best wine last. You have a greater appreciation for the miracle. It wasn't just water that was turned to wine, it was dirty water that was transformed into great tasting wine.

On July 4th, 2020, we woke up to the news that the nation. had broken another daily coronavirus record with more than 57,000 new infections. I remember daily we would monitor the numbers on the morning and evening news because we were looking to see if our prayers to God to reverse this pandemic and its tragic results were working. It was the seventh time in nine days the U.S. reported a new record, and at least 20 states set new highs for the average number of daily new infections over the last seven days. Despite the record-breaking numbers we persisted in prayer believing that we would see the results of our prayer sooner rather than later. Meanwhile, the number of coronavirus cases across the globe surpassed 11 million on the Friday before.

My day started at about 7 am with my personal prayer and devotion. Prayer was and yet remains the center of my communication and life support with God. But it wasn't just my life support, I had a church family that I was determined to keep locked into faith in God, and to have peace during the storm called COVID-19. It's no secret what the pandemic had done to the world at large. Streets and communities were largely abandoned for a spell as most retreated indoors and companies transitioned to online platforms and had employees checking in from their home computers. After my time of personal prayer, I called into a prayer line with prayer warriors and intercessors from around the country. They had the same prayer focus as I did and were believers in the idea that *fervent prayers of the righteous avail much*. During this time, prayer was in the heart, and on the lips of many in the world because of the season of death that the earth was experiencing. However, my commitment to prayer and leading others in prayer helped to stabilize our faith in God through this very arduous and difficult season.

July 4th was a day that was special specifically for the United States of America because it is the day that we celebrate our independence, and typically the smell of BBQ would be in the air. Therefore, after prayer and before heading on my usual morning three-mile prayer walk, I prepared the grill to come back and BBQ for my family. The morning was going, business as usual. The grill was prepped, I had even taken the meat that I was going to grill out of the deep freeze to begin defrosting, and I was dressed to begin my prayer walk. Prayer walks? You may be asking. Didn't I already have my time of personal prayer and devotion, and wasn't that followed up by participation in a prayer call, what more could, and would I do while walking? You and I could never pray too much. The Bible adjures us to, "Pray without ceasing."

This term, which is to be found in 1 Thessalonians 5 means to pray incessantly, without intermission and uninterruptedly. So, this time of walking and being in prayer by myself was not me being obsessive about prayer, but it was me being obedient to the call to prayer. I wanted to fill the empty spaces in my life with communion with God.

Chapter Three
The Prayer Walk that Changed Everything

Jeremiah 29:7
And seek the peace of the city where I have sent you into exile and pray to the Lord on its behalf; for in its peace, you will have peace.

At about 8:03 am EST, I began my three-mile prayer walk. My prayer started well, as I conversed with the Lord. To an outside observer, it may seem like I'm talking to myself, but for me, it's a spiritual conversation. Midway, I joined a prayer call hosted by New Beginnings Church led by Pastor Mary Hoyt. Participants offered prayers of thanksgiving, strategic requests regarding illnesses, and engaged in spiritual warfare. For about two miles of my walk, I listened and prayed along through my earbuds. The call had intercessors from places like Jamaica and California, making it a diverse and powerful session.

I had walked about a mile and the prayer call was ending. As I reached Gate City Boulevard, I encountered my first busy area with potential traffic issues. During COVID-19, streets were usually empty except for occasional squirrels or rabbits. On this street, there was two-way traffic. Walking on the sidewalk, I noticed a car approaching from about 50 yards away and another speeding vehicle moving east to west. Despite their speeds and directions, I felt no fear or panic, as I was aware of where I was heading and did not expect them to cross my path.

The New Beginnings Church Prayer Call was concluding, and I had become more focused in my personal prayers, delving deeper into contemplation. As this occupied my thoughts, two cars approached my location on the sidewalk at a high speed. An unforeseen event occurred when one vehicle, approaching the intersection of Gate City Blvd, failed to observe a stop sign while traveling at approximately 50 miles per hour. It collided with another vehicle headed towards me on Gate City Blvd. The impact was severe, causing the car advancing towards me to lose control. Despite the unfolding events, I remained stationary, unaware of the potential danger. I reassured myself that I would be safe; however, this proved to be incorrect.

The Eyewitness Account

During the events described, there was an eyewitness to it all. Aside from God, another human being observed the situation from a safe distance and was able to contact emergency services, my wife, and the authorities to report the incident. This witness played a crucial role by quickly notifying the necessary parties. At that time, during the COVID-19 pandemic, the streets were mostly deserted as people were staying indoors and practicing social distancing. However, someone was present to see and report the incident, thereby helping to piece together what had happened. This individual, referred to here as Mr. Grant for anonymity, provided detailed observations of the event. He informed my wife, Stacey, saying, "Your husband looked like a rag doll flying high in the air." He emphasized the extraordinary nature of the event and questioned how survival was possible. What followed was an understanding of being supported and sustained through difficult times.

Chapter Four
On Angels Wings Experience

Psalm 91:11
For he will command his angels concerning you to guard you in all your ways.

Hebrews 1:14
Are they not all ministering spirits sent out to serve for the sake of those who are to inherit salvation?

That day, I was struck by a car traveling about 50 mph. Scientific research shows that such an impact often causes severe injuries, including broken bones, organ damage, head trauma, and possibly death. The collision was so intense that I was knocked out of my shoes. I should have died; my body shouldn't have survived such force.

At 50 mph, the risk of fatal injuries is very high. Impacts at this speed can cause severe injuries like broken bones, skull fractures, and internal organ damage. Typically, such injuries occur even with some protection, but this incident involved a defenseless jogger. Normally, such a collision would be fatal, but this case was described as a miracle.

Many would say what happened next is related to going into shock by the impact and trauma your body would experience after such an event. Sustaining the level of physical damage as we described earlier is part of the course for a collision with a vehicle going at those extreme speeds.

However, what happened next for me was supernatural. Nature took its course, but what I experienced was that of being carried on Angels Wings. What looked like shock to those on the outside looking in or at me, saw the usual signs of blunt force trauma. But I was experiencing something completely different.

Physically, there was pain, but spiritually it was painless. In fact, the flight was so profound and supernatural, I felt like I was in a cocoon or in a state of spiritual bliss. I flew approximately 50 feet in the air, according to the eyewitness. Again, I owe it to those who saw it with their own two eyes to tell their story, because only then could it be verified.

I'm reminded of the story of the nation of Israel as they crossed the Red Sea in escape from a pursuing Egyptian Pharaoh and his army. The Bible tells us something interesting that happened in the execution of another miracle. When Israel was escaping the pursuit of the Egyptians and had come to the Red Sea, the Bible tells us that God made a dry path through the sea for the Israelites to escape through. However, I think that little is talked about what else happened.

It says in Exodus 14:19-20, The angel of God who was going before the Israelite army moved and went behind them, and the pillar of cloud moved from in front of them and took its place behind them. **20** It came between the army of Egypt and the army of Israel. And so, the cloud was there with the darkness, and it lit up the night; one did not come near the other all night. God literally placed darkness between the Israelites and their pursuers. The pursuers could only see what they could see. They could see only what God allowed them to see. That day when I was launched out of my shoes into the air, that is what onlookers may have seen and the drivers of those speeding cars, but I was experiencing something completely different.

It felt like hours of transitioning into another realm, confirming that I had entered the spiritual realm. We may touch its edges during passionate worship but being fully immersed as I was rare. It felt like being knocked into another world, possibly by an automobile in the natural world, but truly an angel transporting me to a new reality.

Miracles are hard to prove because they rely on faith and cannot be tested scientifically. However, some believe there's evidence of miracles. A strong example is when people witness events that defy expectations. I was told I was unconscious for about 20 minutes after the accident. The eyewitness expected to report my death but was shocked to find me alive and somewhat conscious.

A miracle, a supernatural act of God without human intervention, occurred when I was lifted by Angels' Wings. This experience was profound, but what made it even more astonishing was being gently placed down in green pastures, which I call my "Psalm 23 Miracle." Lifted into the air on Angel's wings, I was then set down in Green Pastures.

During the temptations of Jesus, the devil urged Him to throw Himself down from a high place, misinterpreting Psalm 91:11-12, which speaks of angels protecting people when it says, **For He shall give His angels charge over you, to keep you in all your ways. In *their* hands they shall bear you up, lest you dash your foot against a stone.** The devil challenged Jesus to prove He was God's Son by acting recklessly. However, true followers of Christ don't need to prove their faith; God sends help in times of danger. Similarly, when I was hit by a car, I believe angels assisted me, ensuring I landed safely.

On The Ground in Green Pastures:

The lift was high, and the drop was fast. I was hit so hard that my sneakers stayed in place. I found myself in a green field, fully aware and praying. My spirit prayed even though I couldn't physically move, as mentioned in Romans 8:26.

As I sang "I am healed by the wound in His Side," which is a song of the legendary Mahalia Jackson, I heard a man, Mr. Anthony Johnson, whom I believe God sent as an "Angel on the Ground," praying and saying, "God is going to heal you." It is a simple song, but it has powerful lyrics, *"I am healed by the wound in His side, oh yes. Oh, they pierced Him in His side. Jesus hung His head and died. I am healed by the wound in His side."* I must have repeated it twice before I heard Mr. Johnson. Although I couldn't move, my faith was strong, and I called out to my Lord through song. Mr. Johnson prayed fervently, thinking I was helpless, but wanting to help. The Bible does say, "The effectual fervent prayer of the righteous avails much." (James 5:16b)

After regaining consciousness on the ground, I realized I had landed within 10 feet of a pond. If I had fallen into the water unconscious, it would have been worse. My left leg was severely twisted, deformed, and broken.

Unable to move, I saw my phone nearby and asked Mr. Johnson to call my wife. I also called my sister, Prophetess Rose Black Henry, who began praying for me. My right leg was severely broken, with all four knee ligaments torn in my left leg, needing surgical repair except one ligament that was supernaturally healing itself. Both sides of my pelvis were cracked, and I had two broken ribs. I couldn't walk or move my legs for months, but prayer kept me alive, and God healed me.

On the afternoon of July 4th, 2020, I arrived at the hospital and underwent surgery. After the procedure, I experienced severe pain and had no mobility from the waist down. During this time, I prayed and worshipped. Over time, I recovered fully and am now able to walk, which I attribute to the effectiveness of prayer and healing practices.

Chapter Five
The Miracle of Movement

Matthew 17:20
Because you have so little faith. Truly I tell you, if you have faith as small as a mustard seed, you can say to this mountain, 'Move from here to there,' and it will move. Nothing will be impossible for you.

The world tilted on its axis. I was walking and praying, the next, a blinding flash of white, the screech of tires, and then, an agonizing silence. My left leg, twisted at an unnatural angle, screamed in agony. Pain, a searing, white-hot inferno, consumed me. I couldn't breathe, I couldn't move. Fear gripped my heart, yet somehow, I clung to whom I believed. The God of all creation.

The blur of sirens, the hushed whispers of the EMTs, the cold steel of the gurney – it all seemed to happen outside of me. I drifted in and out of consciousness, the pain a constant, relentless drumbeat. At the hospital, the news was grim. My left leg, shattered and deformed, seemed beyond repair. The doctors spoke of the severity and complication of the sustained injuries as they viewed the cat-scans. The daunting horror of being confined to a wheelchair was all within reason. My world, vibrant and full of possibilities, shattered like bones within me.

But then, something unexpected happened. Hope, fragile and flickering, began to bloom. Friends and family, bound together by a common thread of faith, rallied around me. Prayers ascended, a symphony of supplication reaching towards heaven. I felt their love, a warm, comforting blanket enveloping me.

The surgeries were brutal because of the possible risk involved, each one a fresh assault on my already weakened body. My right leg, I learned, was severely damaged. The doctors discovered the full extent of the damage to both my left and right legs: not only the shattered bones, but the devastating tear of all four knee ligaments. All except one in my right knee. That one, they said, was healing inexplicably, defying all medical logic.

I remember so clearly that after my very first surgery, laying up in the hospital room in severe pain, I began to weep and worship. In my worship, I remember telling God, "I Choose YOU". I was in pain, but I chose to worship God. In my painful worship experience, I heard the voice of God say, "Bless You". That was all I needed to go on.

Months passed, a slow, agonizing crawl. I lay immobilized, my legs heavy and useless, the weight of despair threatening to crush me. But amidst the pain and frustration, a quiet strength began to grow within me. I clung to the promises whispered in the prayers, the unwavering belief that God was with me, and

He blessed me to go through it. Not just family and friends were praying, but ministry colleagues from far flung places were earnestly going before the Lord on my behalf. In fact, I knew that even relative strangers were praying because that started from the day of the accident, with Mr. Johnson. My sister and the church family held daily prayer vigils on my behalf. It was as though I could feel the very results of those divine probing, I like to think of them. As people prayed, the accumulated effect of their prayers and my faith started to cause physical manifestation of healing in my body.

I am reminded of the story of the four friends and their faith in the Bible is told in the Gospel of Mark, chapter 2. The story is about four friends who carried a paralyzed man to Jesus, even though it meant climbing onto the roof of a house and making a hole. Four friends of a paralyzed man, determined that their friend would see Jesus, dug a hole in the roof and lowered the man on his mat. Jesus, impressed by the faith and tenacity of the paralyzed man and his friends said "Son, your sins are forgiven". Although this wasn't about sins being forgiven, I believe it was about friends and their faith assisting in my healing. The story showed that faith was not just a feeling, but a way of life that involved taking action. Praying is the action that was taken on my behalf. My friends weren't doctors or nurses, or advanced medical professionals but they utilized what they had at their disposal, and that was their faith to pray for my healing. These four friends in the Bible utilized what strength they had and audacity to get their friend before Jesus for help.

Slowly, agonizingly, I began to heal. I remember nights I drifted off to sleep with tears in my eyes, trying to figure out if it was from the pain or from the fatigue that my injured healing body was going through. The bones knit together; the muscles regained their strength. The doctors marveled at the speed of my recovery, the inexplicable healing of that one defiant ligament. They called it a medical anomaly, but I knew better. It was a miracle.

One day, I sat on the edge of the bed, trembling with anticipation. With the help of therapists and family members, I took my first tentative steps. The world, once a distant, unattainable dream, was coming back into focus. Tears streamed down my face, a mixture of joy and gratitude. I had been given a second chance, a gift beyond measure.

My journey back to full recovery was long and arduous. There were setbacks, moments of doubt, and the ever-present whisper of fear. But through it all, I held onto my faith, my belief in the power of prayer, and the unwavering love of those who surrounded me.

Today, I walk again, a testament to the enduring power of the human spirit and the unwavering love of God. The scars remain, both physical and emotional, but they are a reminder of the depths of my suffering and the immeasurable grace that carried me through.

My near-death experience has changed my perspectives of life, faith, and suffering in a very real way. I have experienced sicknesses in my life and physical body before in which God healed me; however, my near-death experience catapulted my faith walk to believe God for the impossible.

According to Hebrews 11:6, the scripture reminds us that "Without faith it is impossible to please God..." In other words, without confidence in the one we cannot see, yet believe, the results and benefits of pleasing Him is futile. Therefore, life impossibilities would be the canvas that God works on to form a quilt of God's faithfulness and sovereign power even during dire circumstances.

When one embraces suffering as a way of God fulfilling His perfect work in mankind. The traumas, road bumps, turns of uncertainty, and "deed sea" experiences, allow our faith to be activated by the consideration God has made for one to experience suffering. Suffering is a triumphant journey towards an unfamiliar path to God's Glory and ultimate victory.

The lesson learned and the experience gained in my near-death experience is that God has the Final Say!

Chapter Six-Closing Message
Sickness is Illegal in my Body, Mind, Soul, and in my Spirit

Take Authority Over the Strong Hold of Sickness and Diseases (in your Body):

Saints of God, we have the power to take authority bind the strong Man and spoil his goods, according to Mark 3:27-29. I believe the Spirit of the Lord has quickened my spirit to remind us at this prayer breakfast that we can take authority over every sickness and disease and walk in victory.

Well, you may ask how do I take authority? It is by declaring the word of God in faith believing and stand firm on it. In other words, do not relent or retreat declare what God said and what Jesus already paid the price for. And do the right thing pertaining to your intake of proper foods

Many have been experiencing an onslaught of sickness, and I feel led this morning to declare to you that you have authority of sickness, and the enemy cannot invade God's territory. When, I begin to feel something trying to happen in my body, I and began to declare the word of God and declare what God already said about me and I then begin to feel the presence of the Lord moving and being activated towards that very thing

Saints, I began to Take Authority Over the Strong Hold of Sickness- not in weakness, rather, by having faith to believe that according to Isaiah 54:17, that No Weapon Formed Against Me Shall Prosper...I feel led to pray the scriptures this morning

Matthew 8: 5-9:
5And when Jesus was entered into Capernaum, there came unto him a centurion, beseeching him,

[6] And saying, Lord, my servant lieth at home sick of the palsy, grievously tormented.

[7] And Jesus saith unto him, I will come and heal him.

[8] The centurion answered and said, Lord, I am not worthy that thou shouldest come under my roof: but speak the word only, and my servant shall be healed.

[9] For I am a man under authority, having soldiers under me: and I say to this man, Go, and he goeth; and to another, Come, and he cometh; and to my servant, Do this, and he doeth it.

Exodus 15: 26- And said, If thou wilt diligently hearken to the voice of the Lord thy God, and wilt do that which is right in his sight, and wilt give ear to his commandments, and keep all his statutes, I will put none of these diseases upon thee, which I have brought upon the Egyptians: for I am the Lord that healeth thee.

Nahum 1:9- What do ye imagine against the Lord? he will make an utter end: affliction shall not rise up the second time.

Luke: 4:40- Now when the sun was setting, all they that had any sick with divers diseases brought them unto him; and he laid his hands on every one of them, and healed them.

2 Chronicles 16:9a- For the eyes of the Lord run to and fro throughout the whole earth, to shew himself strong in the behalf of them whose heart is perfect toward him.

1 Corinthians 2: 9-10:
[9] But as it is written, Eye hath not seen, nor ear heard, neither have entered into the heart of man, the things which God hath prepared for them that love him.
[10] But God hath revealed them unto us by his Spirit: for the Spirit searcheth all things, yea, the deep things of God.

Psalm 34: 19-20:
[19] Many are the afflictions of the righteous: but the Lord delivereth him out of them all.
[20] He keepeth all his bones: not one of them is broken.

Psalm 91: 8-10:
[8] Only with thine eyes shalt thou behold and see the reward of the wicked.
[9] Because thou hast made the Lord, which is my refuge, even the most High, thy habitation;
[10] There shall no evil befall thee, neither shall any plague come nigh thy dwelling.

Mark 16:17-18:
[17] And these signs shall follow them that believe; In my name shall they cast out devils; they shall speak with new tongues;
[18] They shall take up serpents; and if they drink any deadly thing, it shall not hurt them; they shall lay hands on the sick, and they shall recover.

Acts 19: 11-12:

[11] And God wrought special miracles by the hands of Paul:

[12] So that from his body were brought unto the sick handkerchiefs or aprons, and the diseases departed from them, and the evil spirits went out of them.

Acts 5:12-16:

[12] And by the hands of the apostles were many signs and wonders wrought among the people; (and they were all with one accord in Solomon's porch.

[13] And of the rest durst no man join himself to them: but the people magnified them.

[14] And believers were the more added to the Lord, multitudes both of men and women.)

[15] Insomuch that they brought forth the sick into the streets, and laid them on beds and couches, that at the least the shadow of Peter passing by might overshadow some of them.

[16] There came also a multitude out of the cities round about unto Jerusalem, bringing sick folks, and them which were vexed with unclean spirits: and they were healed every one.

Isaiah 53:4-5:
[4] Surely he hath borne our griefs, and carried our sorrows: yet we did esteem him stricken, smitten of God, and afflicted.
[5] But he was wounded for our transgressions, he was bruised for our iniquities: the chastisement of our peace was upon him; and with his stripes we are healed.

James 5:14-15:
[14] Is any sick among you? let him call for the elders of the church; and let them pray over him, anointing him with oil in the name of the Lord:
[15] And the prayer of faith shall save the sick, and the Lord shall raise him up; and if he

have committed sins, they shall be forgiven him.

Other books by this author

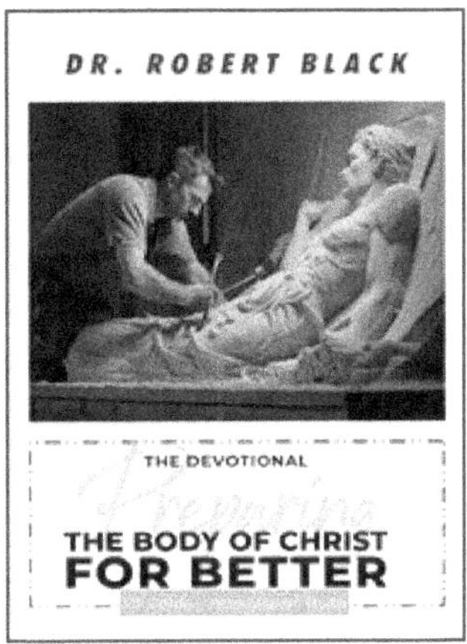

The Responsibility and
Qualifications of a
WORSHIPER
Dr. Robert L. Black
A Manual for Equipping Worship Leaders